Mister and Lady Day

Billie Holiday and the Dog Who Loved Her

AMY NOVESKY

Illustrated by VANESSA BRANTLEY NEWTON

Clarion Books
An Imprint of HarperCollinsPublishers
Boston New York

The text was set in 19 point Primer Print. The illustrations were done in gouache and charcoal on watercolor paper.
The display type was set in Changing and Cocktail Shaker.

The Library of Congress has cataloged the hardcover edition as follows:
Novesky, Amy.
Mister and Lady Day: Billie Holiday and the dog who loved her/Amy Novesky; illustrated by Vanessa Brantley Newton.
p. cm.
I. Mister (Dog)—Juvenile literature. Holiday, Billie, 1915–1959—Juvenile literature. 3. Boxer (Dog breed)—United States—biography—
Juvenile literature. I. Newton, Vanessa, ill. II Title.   ML3930.H64N68 2012   782.42165092—dc23   —[B]—2012025323

ISBN: 978-0-15-205806-7 hardcover   ISBN: 978-0-544-80905-5 paperback

Manufactured in China   SCP 15 14 13 12 11 10 9 8 7 6   4500838422

To Billie and her beloved dogs, to my own beloved George,

and to Samantha, a dedicated editor and friend. Thank you! —A.N.

To Mama Shirley and Pop; we made beautiful music together.

To Coy the Alto, my soprano; love you always.

And thank you to Ha-Shem for your gift of song. —V.B.N.

Billie Holiday loved to sing.
As a girl, she sang along to her favorite songs
on a borrowed gramophone.
She dreamed of being a star . . .

. . . and a star she became—the great Lady Day.

But sometimes stars don't feel like shining.

They need someone to listen.

That's what friends are for.

Lady Day's dogs were her best friends of all.

There were lots of dogs in Lady Day's life:
the poodle she carried in her coat pocket,
and the brown and white beagle.

The Chihuahuas, Chiquita and Pepe, she fed with a baby bottle.

There was the Great Dane named Gypsy,
and the wire-haired terrier Bessie Mae Moocho,
who wagged her tail like a metronome.

Rajah Ravoy, the sad mutt she gave the grandest name, would wander off, but he always found his way home.

And then there was a boxer named Mister.

Mister and Lady Day were rarely apart.

She knit him sweaters and cloaked him in a mink coat.

She cooked for him and took him on midnight walks.

She sang to him.

my baby my sugar

Mister was Lady's favorite.

Someday, she'd have a house in the country filled with dogs.

Life would be good. Mister would be there.

He always was.

When Lady performed at glamorous Harlem clubs,
Mister sat beside her before the show.
Porters brought him plates of thick steak
and bowls of water.

Later he stayed with Lady in her dressing room
while she pinned flowers in her hair.
He kept fans at a polite distance.

When it was time for her to sing,
Mister would lead a nervous Lady to the stage
and wait for her in the wings.

Lady was famous for singing the blues.
But the sadness of her songs didn't matter to Mister

As long as he could hear her, he was happy.

Then, just when her career was at the top, Lady got into trouble.

She had to leave home for a year and a day. And Mister couldn't come.

Lady knew what it was like to be left, and it made her heartsick.

She promised Mister she'd be home soon.

But when she looked into his sad eyes,
she wasn't sure she'd ever see him again.

While Lady was gone, she wrote letters
and knit sweaters. But she did not sing.
Singing was about feeling, and she didn't feel a thing.

When it was finally time to return,
she wondered if Mister would be there.
Would he remember her at all?

Then there he was!

Running down the platform, Mister leaped on Lady,

knocking her down. Someone screamed and everyone scattered.

But soon a crowd gathered. "It's Billie Holiday!"
And Lady's homecoming was as bright
as a paparazzo's flashbulb.

Lady couldn't go home just yet.

On the front porch at a friend's farm, she rehearsed.

It was time for her to sing again, whether she felt like it or not.

In just ten days, she'd have her biggest show ever—
at New York City's Carnegie Hall.

Lady was afraid. She'd heard the rumor that the great
Billie Holiday was through. Was it true?

On the night of the big show, the concert hall glowed.
At midnight, the houselights dimmed and a spotlight
as full as the moon appeared.

Slowly, Lady walked to center stage — the hall so quiet
you could hear her heels click.

Lady trembled.
Where was Mister? Was he waiting in the wings?
As the band's notes began, Lady lifted her chin.
And when the great Billie Holiday sang . . .

And i'm thinking,

. . . everyone and a dog
held their breath and listened.

If you were mine,
i'd never let you go.

BILLIE HOLIDAY (April 7, 1915–July 17, 1959)

was one of the greatest jazz singers who ever lived. She did not have a big voice like some of her contemporaries. Instead, Billie's voice was delicate and bittersweet. She loved sad songs and sang them with great feeling. Throughout her career, she was known as Lady Day—a name given to her by one of her closest friends, jazz musician Lester Young. In addition to being a breathtaking singer, Billie had an arresting sense of style. Big, fragrant gardenias framed her face and a proud dog was often by her side.

Despite achieving fame, Billie's life was not always a happy one. When she was a girl, her father abandoned her, and her mother worked away from home, leaving Billie behind. As an adult, she suffered from a drug addiction and, at the peak of her career, was sentenced to one year in prison for drug possession. While she was gone she refused to sing, because, she said, "I didn't feel a thing." But on March 27, 1948, just days after her homecoming, she performed a sold-out show at New York City's prestigious Carnegie Hall before a crowd of thousands. So many people came to see her sing, in fact, that extra seats were added on the stage. Billie performed more than thirty songs and wore not just one dress, but changed into another at intermission, pinning her signature white flowers in her hair. In spite of her troubles—troubles that would follow her until the day she died at age forty-four—the great Lady Day shone like a star that memorable night.

Whether Mister attended this performance is not documented, but he was by Lady's side at other venues, keeping her company and calming her before she sang. The story's last line is inspired by a famous poem called "The Day Lady Died" by Frank O'Hara, and the lyrics that follow it are from the song "But Beautiful." Additional lyrics are from the song "Sugar."

To learn more about Billie Holiday's life and music, visit **www.billieholiday.com.**

SOURCES

Clarke, Donald. *Wishing on the Moon: The Life and Times of Billie Holiday.* New York: Viking, a division of Penguin Putnam, 1994.

Holiday, Billie, with William Dufty, foreword by David Ritz. *Lady Sings the Blues.* New York: Doubleday, a division of Random House, Inc., 1956.

Kliment, Bud. *Billie Holiday (Black Americans of Achievement).* New York: Chelsea House Publications, 1990.

O'Meally, Robert. *Lady Day: The Many Faces of Billie Holiday.* Cambridge, Mass.: Da Capo Press, 1991.